Plusman eats a lot..

A STEM with Me series begins!

Dharini Mohanraj

BLUEROSE PUBLISHERS
India | U.K.

Copyright © Dharini Mohanraj 2023

All rights reserved by author. No part of this publication may be reproduced, stored in a retrieval system or transmitted in any form or by any means, electronic, mechanical, photocopying, recording or otherwise, without the prior permission of the author. Although every precaution has been taken to verify the accuracy of the information contained herein, the publisher assumes no responsibility for any errors or omissions. No liability is assumed for damages that may result from the use of information contained within.

BlueRose Publishers takes no responsibility for any damages, losses, or liabilities that may arise from the use or misuse of the information, products, or services provided in this publication.

For permissions requests or inquiries regarding this publication,
please contact:

BLUEROSE PUBLISHERS
www.BlueRoseONE.com
info@bluerosepublishers.com
+91 8882 898 898
+4407342408967

ISBN: 978-93-5819-477-7

Cover design: Muskan Sachdeva
Typesetting: Pooja Sharma

First Edition: December 2023

This book belongs to

Dedicated to my lovely daughters who motivated me to develop my story-telling skills by haunting me for stories! Dedicated to my husband who believes in me always!

I'm elated to start this journey as a new author. As one who has closely worked with early years and preschoolers, I've always been fascinated by the power of storytelling and interactive read-aloud. As a mom of two, I've experienced the wonder of story that influence children in their conceptual learning and thus STEM concepts become easier and more effective.

I'm here, channelling my passion into my debut book "Plusman eats a lot".

A STEM with me series begins!

In a cozy town cuddled between the foothills,
a little superhero named
Plusman lived.

This superhero wasn't like other common superheroes who had unbelievable strength. Instead, he had a special power
--the power of addition!

Plusman had a big heart and an even bigger appetite. He loved eating, and he loved helping people around him. He spent his days whizzing around the town, looking for ways to use his special power.

He loved counting the people he saw.
He loved counting every single bite he ate. He loved counting birds and cars, and it goes on!

Plusman had a big heart and an even bigger appetite. He loved eating, and he loved helping people around him.

He spent his days whizzing around the town, looking for ways to use his special power.

Every time he counted those people he saw, he ate a mug of cake baked at the shop.

"Oh, there's Miss Meow, the cat lady, at number 5! You see, Plusman eats a lot…." he said, gulping his fifth mug of carrot cake.

One sunny morning, Plusman was enjoying his favorite breakfast of mug cake. As he relished each mouthful, the owner of the bakery, Mr. Mond, the baker, rushed in. He seemed to be worried.

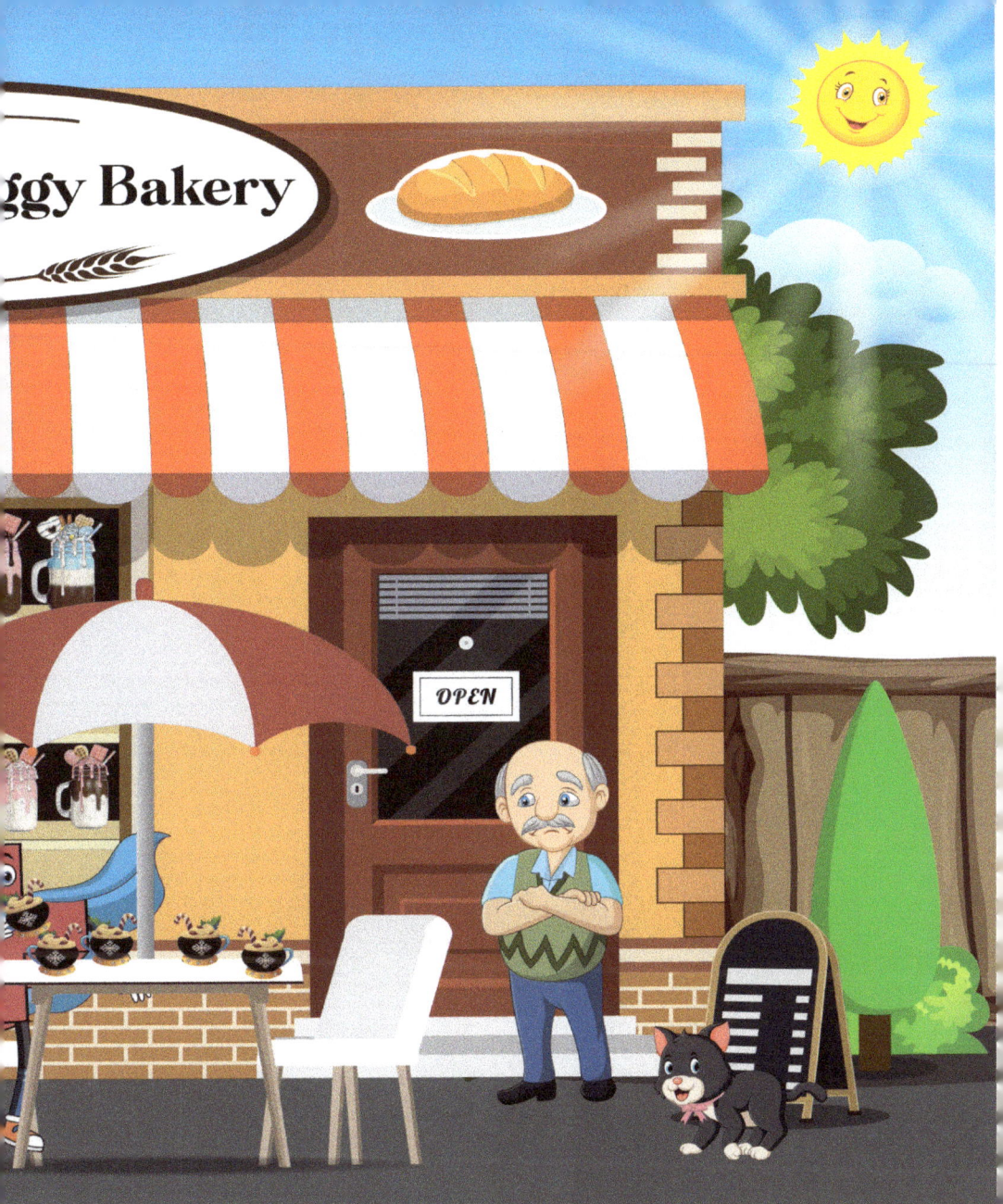

"Plusman, I think I'm in trouble", he whined. "I don't have enough ingredients to bake a sufficient number of carrot mug cakes for the town's bake sale!"
Plusman knew the way. "Don't worry, Mr. Mond! I'm here to help you. Just tell me what you need."

Mr. Mond passed him a list of ingredients. "To make carrot mug cakes, I need 3 cups of flour, 2 cups of sugar, and 3 cups of grated carrots."

Nodded our superhero Plusman and sped with his three feet!

He visited the local grocery store and gathered 3 cups of flour, 2 cups of sugar, and 3 cups of grated carrots. With each item he picked up, he mumbled the numbers, working on his addition skills. He gathered all the ingredients and sped back to the bakery.

Mr. Mond was relieved to see a bag full of ingredients Plusman brought to him. "You've got everything!" he marveled.

Plusman proudly declared, "And I've got something else too – My calculator brain!"

He spread the ingredients on the table and began to add them up. "3 cups of flour, 2 cups of sugar, and 3 cups of grated carrots equal…

He tapped his chin, counting on his fingers.

"8 mugs of heavenly carrot cakes, that's my favorite!" mumbling and chuckling and humming, "You see, Plus-man eats a lot!" Mr. Mond was thrilled and said "Plus-man! You're amazing".

Everyone gathered, and with his power of addition, Plusman helped Mr. Mond in preparing enough carrot mug cakes to fill the bake sale table.

He also helped Mr. Mond set the table for the sale. The residents were astounded by Plusman's skills and they deeply appreciated his efforts.

Plusman proudly stood next to Mr. Mond, wearing a baker's hat and apron. The carrot mug cakes sold like hotcakes, and Plusman shone brighter as he realized the power of his addition skills.

Plusman took credit for solving a baking puzzle and proved to everyone that addition could be fun and valuable in everyday life. From that day on, Plusman became the town's adored superhero, using his super-addition skills to help in all kinds of situations.

That night, Plusman relished his eighth mug of carrot cake and muttered, "You see, Plusman eats a lot." "And you got a lot of heart too…" mumbled Mr. Mond, offering Plusman his ninth mug of cake.

Not an end! It was just the beginning of Plusman's adventures in helping others with his special abilities.

www.ingramcontent.com/pod-product-compliance
Lightning Source LLC
LaVergne TN
LVHW061628070526
838199LV00070B/6619